I am the Black Woman

R. N. HEADLAM

Independently Published by R. N. Headlam

Printed by Amazon, LLC in the United States of America

First Publication: 2022

Cover Designer: The Pink Ravyn

For more information on other books and inquiries, please visit:

www.thepinkravyn.com

Table of Contents

FOREWORD

Ever since heading off to college, I found myself in quite a predicament. I had no idea who I really was.

I spent a good portion of my college years trying to piece together who I was. I searched all over, but came up with nothing. However, throughout those years I found a friend who helped me understand who I really was. I could tell you countless stories—miracles that came my way, helping me to put together the pieces of the mirror that shattered many years ago.

In my last year of college, I wanted to write a book—a free book that I could include with my fashion illustration portfolio that would give some idea of the collection. I never got to finish that book in time, but I still had the idea in mind.

So, when I began scanning through a few things that I had, I realized I had enough content to put together a short prose and poetry—the one that you're currently holding in your hand and reading.

It's a collection of twenty-six wonderful poems and proses that I'm sure will inspire you. It's all about my journey as a Black woman coming to the U.S. But, it's more than that.

In 2021, I embarked on a journey to write a novel called *The Aroma of Rain,* which I'll hopefully have published in 2023 (fingers crossed). I decided to include four full-chapter excerpts from the book, hoping that you will enjoy those excerpts enough to come back for more.

Given that these excerpts are in their final stages, it's not quite complete. However, I did my best to clean them up for your reading pleasure.

I do hope you enjoy the wonders, the laughter, and the tears that this book brings to you.

A Virtuous Woman

Who can find a virtuous woman? For her worth is far above rubies. The heart of her husband can safely trust in her. He will have no lack of gain. She does him good and not evil all the days of her life.

She seeks wool and flax and willingly works with her hands. She is like the merchant ships who brings her food from afar. She rises while it is still night and provides food for her household and a portion for her maidservants. She considers a field and buys it. From her profits she plants a vineyard.

She girds herself with strength, and she strengthens her arms. She perceives that her merchandise is good. Her lamp does not go out by night. She stretches out her hands to the distaff, and her hand holds the spindle.

She extends her hand to the poor. Yes, she reaches out her hands to the needy. She is not afraid of snow for her household is clothed with scarlet. She makes tapestry for herself. Her clothing is fine linen and purple. Her husband is known in the gates when he sits among the elders of the land. She makes linen garments and sells them and supplies sashes for the merchants.

Strength and honor are her clothing; she shall rejoice in time to come. She opens her mouth with wisdom and her tongue is the law of kindness. She watches over the ways of her household and does not eat the bread of idleness. Her children rise up and call her blessed; her husband also, and he praises her:

"Many daughters have done well, but you excel them all."

Charm is deceitful and beauty is passing, but a woman who fears the Lord, she shall be praised. Give her of the fruit of her lands and let her own works praise her in the gates.

Proverbs 31:10-31

Who Am I?

I am the jewel that many men search for
A diamond hard to find
I am the precious stone among many rocks
The radiant beam of sunshine
I am the tree that stands tall by the river banks
While the storm takes the others away
I am the woman worth fighting for
The woman who will never stray

I am the precious gold among the dust
The sweetest fruit on the highest limb of the tree
I am the rare corals in the ocean's depth
And the valuable shells beneath the sea
I am the tides that come and go
I am the light of the moon
And where others die and wither away
There is where I bloom

I am the rose among all the thorns
I am the hill in the midst of valleys
I am the crown worn on the king's head
And the gold paved street among alleys
I do not take the paths that others take
But walk where there is none
And there is where I leave a trail
So that others may follow on

I am not a princess who needs a prince
Nor do I need to be saved by a knight
I am a queen who runs her own kingdom
A kingdom where there is no war nor fight
I have saved many and I have saved myself
I am in no need of a savior or guide
I am a leader in my own palace
And a hero to my own tribe

When others fall and many fade
I shine brighter than even the sun
When others fail and their journeys end
I know that mine has just begun
And with each word in this poem
This is what I know and where I stand
That I have a cause inside of me
Because this is who I am

Spoken Word

*Let someone else praise you, and not your own mouth;
an outsider, and not your own lips.*

Proverbs 27:2

Why Am I Black?

In my fifth semester of college, I essentially asked God the same question RuNett Ebo asked: *Why did you make us Black?*

He began to compare the Black race to soil—and He answered the question beautifully:

"You are made in My image. And in My image, I made you with soil—dirt. Many people, when they look at dirt, they think it is worthless. Dirt is spat on, trampled on, kicked aside, and thought of as nothing. But what they don't realize is that the very dirt they kick is the foundation this Earth is built upon.

"Look around. Everything you see on this planet comes from the soil. The food you eat needs the soil in order to grow. The houses you build comes from the dirt, and then they are set into the dirt as a foundation to help them stand.

"All the gold and diamonds are minded in the dirt. The oil that fuels your Earth is found several feet below the dirt. The very minerals needed to create your technology are found in the soil. Everything you need is in the dirt, and without the dirt, the Earth you know wouldn't exist today. Yet, so many people take the dirt for granted and think of it as worthless. But this soil is the most valuable thing on this planet. Because the things you value comes from it.

"You are Black just like Me. You are undervalued, spat upon, trampled upon, and cast aside, but they don't know that you are the very foundation of this civilization. They do the same to Me, even now. They say I don't exist, I am worthless, I am just the figment of some man's imagination, corrupt, evil, and egotistical. The same they say about you. But I know the truth. I am the very foundation this universe was built upon. I am the very essence of life. From Me, all good things became.

"And thus, I made you, the Black Woman in My image.

"The human race was born in Africa: traced back to a single Black Woman who gave birth to all the civilizations today. Without you, there would be no humans, so civilization.

"The Black Man symbolizes power, authority, strength, and wisdom. They try to take that away, but the Black Man is made in My image. The Black Woman is made in My image.

"So, they may trample on you, spit on you, call you worthless, ignore you, undervalue you; don't pay them any mind. You know the truth. So when the Earth trembles and humans realize how everything they've created can come shattering down with just an earthquake, one day their foundation will shake, and they will understand just how important you are.

"You are Black. You are made in My image. You are made in the image of God."

True Freedom

True freedom comes from within.

One cannot hope to find freedom in a place or within a person. One cannot hope to find freedom when they've achieved all their goals. One cannot even hope to find freedom when they have all they could be given.

One chooses to be free.

Freedom is a state of mind. It is found within the depths of our souls. Freedom remembers humility; freedom is servitude.

Freedom is not a place we can go but rather a place we should become. We don't abide in freedom: freedom abides in us. Freedom is love. Freedom is truth. Freedom is sacrifice. Freedom can never leave: it can never disappear.

Freedom is the state of all things.

Where there is hope, where there is joy, where there is peace, where there is love, there is freedom. Freedom cannot be defined by words, for we are the definition of freedom. We understand pain and sorrow, hopelessness and despair; thus, we understand the nature of freedom.

In bondage, we found hope. In shackles, we found love. In chains, we found joy. On plantations, we found promise. In despair, we found destiny. And within our hearts, we found freedom.

We broke the shackles, untied the ropes, united, and resisted. We became strong, we became power, and we became freedom.

We found love...

...And only in love can we be in bondage and still be free.

This is freedom.

Death
EXCERPT #1

I didn't come here to watch the ones who I loved die. That's simply not what I came here to do, but no matter how much I tried to wipe the tears away, they kept coming. They came, drowning my face as I pressed my back against a boulder—the only comfort I had.

After spending eons rethinking the first choice I'd made, I came here because I did not like to see people die.

When humans had cut the strings between themselves and the Triune, they essentially cut themselves away from me—and for that, they became mortal. I'd promised Yah on the day it had happened that I'd find a way to relink us back to the humans. And I wrote myself into Earth's fate: wrote the story. Generations had come and gone since I'd made that choice.

I'd taken those years to decide whether I actually wanted to do it, especially since Yo had told me that if I did become human, I would have to die. But I was immortal—I couldn't die. And even if I could—death—I hated it.

I did not want to die.

I spent endless generations trying to figure out ways to avoid it, but alas, if I wanted to complete the story I'd written for Earth, I had to live as a human. I had to die as a human. I was faced with the reality that this was my fate. There was no way to avoid it; I swallowed an old breath in exchange for a new one—the first breath as a human.

But now, some nineteen years after that breath, here I was crying because once again, someone I loved had died.

He was killed right in front of me and I did nothing. I could do nothing. I couldn't even kiss his face goodbye and tell him how much he meant to me. He was my father—the one who raised me from birth as his. He was the one who taught me and encouraged me, and now, he was gone. Gone all because of what the ancient humans did.

His soul had nowhere to go.

I didn't want to go back to the place to find his body. I didn't even know what direction I ran. Going back there meant I would have to face the men who took his life. I knew they were on the lookout, anticipating my return so that they could take my life too.

And I couldn't go home.

What would I tell my *Ima*? That I just watched her husband get murdered? I was the son. I was supposed to defend him; I should have done something. Fight back. Offer up my life. But I didn't—I couldn't.

I. Hated. Death.

Though the power of death was the very essence of my core—my power. Though I was the author of everyone's fate. Though I was the one who determined when a life took their first breath—and their last. I hated death.

It was the reason why I made this planet—to escape death. Here was supposed to be a place where no one died, but when the wind struck its chord and humans untethered themselves from us, there was nothing I could do but watch them die.

The cold air swept the sand in my face; the night sky had nothing in it but a few twinkling lights that didn't help me see my surroundings any better. I pulled myself off the ground. I had no food nor water, so it made no sense for me to stay here. And I couldn't go back to retrieve what I'd left behind.

"Everything serves its purpose," I remembered *Ima* saying the day we attended Zachariah's funeral.

At the time, I was only seven years old. I was too young to understand what she'd meant by that. But now that I was older and the memories that were once concealed now revealed themselves, I knew exactly what she meant. Underneath these stars, I could not tell why Yosef had to die—his fate was written eons before he was even born.

But I was sure above these stars, there was a perfectly good reason why he had to die.

Wade in the Water

Wade in the water, children
God is gonna trouble these waters

In today's world, many Black people are beginning to wake up and recognize their history and where they come from. This is a good thing. In fact, this should be celebrated on all accounts.

However, the most traumatic thing to learn is that during the Transatlantic Slave Trade, many of my ancestors died. They died on the vessels that carried them to the Americas, on the plantations, and during the revolts that eventually led to their freedom.

Many people seem to think that because of how they died and the corruption caused by the white plantation owners during those days, that Christianity was forced on us as Black people. This is true to an extent, but here goes nothing.

My ancestors were bought, stolen, and kidnapped from West Africa to work on plantations. They already had their own spiritual beliefs and religion, which can be seen today in Africa and the Americas.

When they landed in the Americas, two schools of thought arose. Some planters believed because West Africans were 'heathen,' it was justifiable to enslave them, and then there were planters who believed that 'converting' them would make them more docile and willing to work.

Of the Africans who were forced to convert, the planters did everything in their power to stagnate their spiritual beliefs and the way the Africans wanted to worship.

At the time, there were significantly more planters who believed the first school of thought: that African heathenism was grounds to justify slavery. In Europe, most civilians were unaware of what was taking place in the Americas and didn't even know about the cruelties happening to West Africans.

When some of the churches in Europe learned of what was taking place in the Americas, they were outraged, claiming that slavery was against Christian doctrine. However, many other Christians (especially those who were slave owners at the time) began to use religion to justify slavery. In fact, they used religion to justify racism.

The topics they used to justify what they did included teaching Africans that they were descendants of Ham and that they were cursed, even claiming that slavery was necessary to carry out God's will. They taught this doctrine to the enslaved Africans to keep them submissive.

However, other Christian missionaries were completely against this and made a point to set up churches in the Americas to teach the Africans to read (this came in handy in reading slave bills) and fight for their freedom. Nevertheless, all these opinions were still the opinions of white Europeans and not necessarily the opinions of those who were actually suffering: the African slaves.

So, what did the slaves do?

They found a way to identify with the religion and mix their understanding of spiritual things with this newfound faith. After reading the Bible and finding identity with the teachings of Christ and the Israelites when they were in captivity, many of them took the religion and began to use it to enlighten other slaves, encouraging them to join in with the rebellion.

Even the well-loved Negro Spirituals that many Black Christians sing today were written by the Africans in direct opposition to white culture and politics.

An example of this is the Spiritual, 'Nobody Knows the Trouble I've Seen,' which speaks of the hardships many slaves bore on the plantation. 'Wade in the Water' is another Spiritual based on the Exodus of the Israelites out of Egypt. It is also believed that the song contained a hidden meaning to fugitive slaves that enabled them to avoid recapture.

These messages had hidden meanings and took inspiration from West African music, culture, and spirituality. They were lyrics that spoke of the hardship the slaves bore and their opposition to the planters who enslaved them. These songs helped to form their rebellion.

Today, we consider the most successful rebellion to be the Haitian Revolution, the first country to have slavery abolished, and the first country to have done so through a slave rebellion. This successful rebellion is credited to Toussaint Louverture, the general who led it.

Louverture was a slave until 1776, before he led the rebellion that would abolish slavery in Haiti. He was a well-educated man. His work in the slave rebellion found its inspiration in several different social issues, including his background as a Catholic who believed that slavery was against the teachings of the Church and that freedom was every man's God-given right.

Another person who comes to mind is Samuel Sharpe, an enslaved Jamaican and Baptist deacon who led the slave rebellion known as the Baptist War (Christmas Rebellion). He led this uprising during a time when missionary rebels and abolitionists were learning of a supposed bill that would abolish slavery. Several churches organized protests and strikes, and Sharpe's church was one of them.

The Christian faith has been heavily scrutinized among the Black community as it relates to the church's role in slavery, and this scrutiny comes with good and sound logic. After all, Christian planters used the Bible and the religion to justify their actions. However, the great thing about my ancestors was that they were able to take a religion (meant to keep them docile), study it, and learn that their beliefs can be used to actually empower and free them.

My ancestors were the ones who used this very religion to liberate the enslaved Africans by finding their identity in it. Even so, they were able to regain and reconnect to a form of worship that was authentic and unique to them, finding its roots in West African culture and bringing it to a society that tried to destroy it.

Many religions have been morally grey throughout history: having been persecuted or being the persecutor. Many religious scriptures and holy books have been interpreted, reinterpreted, and even misinterpreted to fit a bias or personal agenda.

It doesn't matter to what religion someone belongs or doesn't belong. It matters right now our hearts, thinking, and willingness to learn from past mistakes and do better. It matters our understanding of our history and what we can do to create an atmosphere of love, peace, joy, and unity.

No one should be scrutinized, hated, or discredited for their beliefs. No one should be indoctrinated and forced to believe something. We all are given free will to believe as we want. We all should have a right to freedom: freedom to live, freedom to learn, freedom to believe, freedom to excel and grow.

Freedom is what my ancestors fought for. Freedom is what should be encouraged.

Freedom is what should be celebrated.

A Colder Fire

"How much more do you want?" he questions.

"Just enough to keep this fire burning. It doesn't make any sense to stop now." She sighs. "I'm not sure if we belong together. I love you, and you love me, but you're a—demon. I can't be with you."

He turns to look at her, but she can't see his eyes. It's hidden within the shadow cast by his hood. "If we were meant to be together, we'll be together," he consoles. "Why do you worry? Why don't you trust me? Do you think that loving me will send you to hell?"

She looks up from the campfire that they made, then she sighs. Her heart tells her they belong together—it's what she believed for a very long time. "If you only knew how much I love you," she softly says, holding back the tears that threatened to flow. "But if you only knew what this would do to me."

No matter what she says to him, it is as though he refuses to understand. But he has to. How does he expect a girl like her to marry someone like him?

There were times she'd pray that he wasn't who he was. That he was someone else. If he were, maybe she would consider marrying him, but she couldn't just put herself with anyone in this reality. It didn't matter to them that she was in love.

It isn't her intention to hurt him, but leaving him is the best option she has. If anything happens, her soul will be saved—but it means his soul will be chained to hell eternally. Can love truly save him? Or is it all just a figment of her imagination? Is it her desperate search to be accepted? So much so that she finds solace in the love of a demon? Madness. The only way that could ever happen is if they were the last two people on Earth.

And even then, she will have to tread carefully. Her soul is at its last string with the angels. He has no excuse to give them, but they are willing to take a chance on her. Maybe he is trying to use her to get back into heaven. But if love insists, and she sees that her heart still yearns for him the way the river yearns for the ocean, then she knows her love is true.

If he can journey to find her heart, then she knows his love is true.

She can never be with him, but she can pray. Her prayer can rise to the heavens, to the angels. And at least, if her prayers are not answered, and he goes to hell, she will pray that God would place him in a colder fire.

Everyone Needs Love

Every once in a while, we forget that everyone needs a little love to make it through the day, but not everyone gets it.

Unfortunately, we are so caught up in our own ways that we fail to realize the others who are hurting even more than ourselves. Our selfish ways of thinking and the greed of having it all often come between our desires and other people's needs.

We judge people based on their outward appearances and forget that people have a much deeper reason for being who they are. We fail to see the person on the inside because we are so busy looking at the person outside.

Do you know what I learned? I learned that some people struggle to find themselves. They struggle to find a purpose in life, and because of this, they ever so often give up.

They think their life is meaningless. They lost the sense of being loved and being able to fall in love. What is even more heartbreaking is that these people don't always understand what they're going through; they feel like they're being judged through the tainted lenses of people who are indeed judging them.

There is one thing I'm sure of: people who hurt the most are the ones who give their all to save others. Deep down inside, they are good creatures; they are angels sent from heaven to help us on our journey through.

There are many angels among us.

Many good-hearted people sit among us, but they don't want to be here. They hate it on the Earth because people ill-treat them. Sometimes they 'lash out,' and because of this, they are told they are bad people.

They are the outcasts in society, and all they desire is to fit in. Many don't even dare to let others know how they feel because they are so used to saving others that they believe they cannot be saved.

They blame themselves for the condition they're stuck in; they go through a lot. They suffer a lot of spiritual turmoil. They are underappreciated, and they are taken advantage of. They sit in their private rooms and cry all night because their pain is so intense that there is nothing else to stop it.

When all is said and done, they come back out with a smile as though nothing happened. They live behind lies and often try as much to not make anyone feel hated. That's why they try so hard to please other people and forget to please themselves.

They give the best advice and encouragement to those who don't need it, but often neglect themselves though they know what they go through.

These 'angels' need a home. Not a physical home, but a spiritual home. They need to find a place of peace. They need to be around people who have seen their problems yet love them unconditionally and promise to do anything to make their stay on Earth as comfortable as possible.

These angels don't need materialistic gifts. They just need to be reminded that their life has a purpose: that they made someone smile. That they fulfilled the duty they came on Earth to do. That they, in fact, have loved and have received love. That they are seen as heroes.

These 'angels' don't need prayer. They need love.

Their affection needs to be returned. They don't ask for much, but the thing is that they are too afraid to ask at all. So, I have found out that their words say one thing, but their heart begs to differ. What their heart wants is a place to rest. A tamer who can calm the rage they feel within, the sadness they have hidden inside, and their rejection.

They might be different. They might not fit into social standards. They might struggle with their identity because they never really fit in anywhere. But if we can give them a place where they are treated like a normal person, if we can show them that they fit perfectly within our hearts, and if we can show them their identity, we can make these angels smile.

And you know what? They will never want to leave Earth. Because Earth is like their second home. They will willingly accept their flaws, but they will know that they still love and are still loved.

They will never turn their backs on us. They will never cry, they will never feel pain, they will never struggle to fit in, and ultimately, they will never try to escape Earth. They will spread their wings once more and fly. And by flying, they will carry us on their wings.

What is Love?

Love is patient and kind;

Love does not envy or boast; it is not arrogant or rude.

It does not insist on its own way;

It is not irritable or resentful;

It does not rejoice at wrongdoing but rejoices with the truth.

Love bears all things, believes all things, hopes all things, and endures all things.

1 Corinthians 13:4-7

The Doll

The day I lost my doll, everything changed…

I was just a young girl, somewhere between six and eight, when I received my first Black Barbie doll. It was a collector's item.

She was different from the other dolls I had. She wasn't the standard 'blue-eyed-blonde-hair' Barbies I'd owned, which were all in despicable condition. She was brand new. She came in a large, pink dress; she had dark brown eyes, dark hair, and a wide smile. But then, I took her to school, loaned her to a 'friend,' and never got her back.

And everything changed.

I loved that doll. I didn't know it then, but I know it now. She was different with a lovely smile and a gorgeous dress. Her existence motivated me to pursue design as a career. There was something about her, but at the time when I had her, I never understood her value.

I understand her value now.

You see, Black Barbie dolls were a rare sight. Everywhere I turned, white dolls were prevalent. When I was young, my mother made an effort to ensure that I was diverse in my toys. And ever since, that diversity stuck.

My mother had gone out of her way to buy me a prestigious Collector's Black Barbie doll, but I never saw the value in it at the time. I thought it was 'just another toy'. Even though I loved her, I never realized how much she meant until I lost her.

My mother would say, *'the cow never know the use of its tail until it lose it'* (in Jamaican patois). It means that sometimes, we take the things we have for granted, not understanding their purpose and significance until they're lost.

In this case, the 'tail' was a part of my identity—the fact that I'm a Black Caribbean woman. Since then, I have made a conscious effort to retain my identity. I was determined that I wouldn't lose who I was just to fit in with who others wanted me to be.

It was an endearing journey, to say the least.

Throughout fashion school, I've had some challenging times trying to figure out whether I should stick to my gut or I change what I was doing. There were times when I did (it worked out quite well), and there were times when I didn't (which also worked out, but at the expense of my happiness).

I decided that who I am and who I represent were far more important than who others wanted me to be.

The Black Empire

What is nephilology?

It's the study of nephilim: the offspring of angels and human beings.

The nephilim race began hundreds of thousands of years ago when the human race was still young. Biblically, the first appearance of nephilim was documented before the birth of Noah, and they were labeled as giants. However, some people believed that Cain's descendants were nephilim as they claimed he was married to Lilith, a demoness.

Whether Cain's children were nephilim or the first nephilim was around Noah's time remains unclear, but one thing is sure. We are all related to them in some way.

Noah was indeed special because it was believed he was the only remaining purebred human. Many are not sure whether his wife or children were also genetically pure, though there are hints that allude to this truth. After digging much deeper, it became clear that ethnicity was probably the result of nephilim.

The truth might just be that Black Africans are the closest we will ever get to a genetically pure human.

As a matter of fact, scientists have discovered that among all the ethnic diversions, African DNA is made up of almost all human-originated DNA, whereas other ethnicities share DNA with other human-like (neanderthal) species. And here goes the beginning of this short prose.

The Nephilim Empire.

I can start from Noah and go back or start from Noah and go forward, but I think I'd like to start with us and stay here. You might learn a thing or two about yourself.

Racism.

The first form of control. Was it only confined to black and white, or was there something deeper than that?

After the media has spewed lies to each side, I reckon that the world isn't as bad as we were told.

Racial discrimination began when the Europeans thought of themselves as more god-like than the Africans. But could it be embedded in a hatred that caused us to separate even from the days of Noah?

God preferred His human creation over His angelic one, even going as far as giving them their own kingdom to dominate. He created an earth and gave it to humankind to control, much like how He controlled the heavens.

As a popular story suggests, one angel wanted to take over the universe God created only to be kicked out of heaven. But if you truly looked at the story, you would know that these fallen angels were given their own realm to dominate. One with unending darkness.

These angels adopted evil, not because they wanted to control heaven, but because they never thought humans were fit to rule an entire kingdom. Jealousy became the force that drove the fallen angels to attack God and His human creation.

That jealousy turned into greed for power, and that greed fueled a war. Then, that war spilled over on the human race: one between the descendants of nephilim and the descendants of humans. The nephilim stole power from the humans and made it their own, believing themselves to carry on their forefathers' legacy. Thus, the race war began.

This race war spilled over into Europeans taking Africans as their slaves. Taking everything they knew to belong to the Africans, they turned it into a Eurocentric stereotype that anything stemming from Africa was evil and corrupt. The Africans rebelled, but in a way, that made them worse than their European masters.

The Europeans didn't believe that the Africans could become anything. But little did they know that God, the Creator of heaven and Earth, described the color of His skin as burnished brass—the darkest complexion that reflected the Africans.

Once upon a time, humans were in charge of this Earth. They had a Divine Being whose only concern was for the benefit of the entire human race. He sent his only son to be ill-treated and killed to shed his blood for the restoration of a race that was purely human. It meant saving even the descendants of the nephilim.

So, what really ignited racism? Jealousy? Resentment? Greed? What was it?

I believe, and I know you will too, that it all stems from a person's heart. It isn't a universal issue—it is an individual issue that we all suffer from. We all hold a bias. The humans held a bias because they were not like angels. The angels held a bias because they were not like humans.

Though there were Europeans who tortured Africans day and night, there were many who stood side by side with the Africans, fighting for their right to live as free men and women. Some humans put aside their biases to help angels, as Lot did. Some angels put aside their biases to help the humans, as Christ did.

Each person holds a bias. Some of us let our anger and rage hurt innocent people, while others are motivated by the belief that no matter the complexion, we are all equally human and deserve to be treated as such.

So, to those who suffer at the hands of another race, one bad apple does not necessarily spoil the entire bunch. If that were true, we would never shop at supermarkets.

You just have to pick out the good ones and keep them by your side, praying every day that God will show you who they are inside. After all, whether you are Black, White, or Asian, we are human, and in all ways, we are loved by the God who created us all.

Industry

The fashion industry has become a deadly place to call home.

Throughout the course of time, the fashion industry has produced shows that dehumanized, insulted, sexualized, objectified, and even mocked the models they employ.

However, with a turn in social issues, the fashion industry fails to catch up. The industry is easily losing marketability; thus, one can see why many brands are doing their best to 'appear' inclusive. The year 2020 has proven that the fashion industry will only support Black women and other minorities when they can capitalize on it.

'Black Lives Matter' and 'We Stand with You' were shouted from the rooftops of many fashion labels, but these same labels have a history of cultural appropriation, body shaming, racial insensitivity, and misogyny.

Many of these so-called 'woke' fashion brands are elbow-deep in discrimination. They fail to hire Black models, refuse to hire Black designers to work on their teams, Europeanize non-white culture, and produce collections that fetishize Black culture.

The fashion industry needs to change, and we all know it.

The western world has a warped and twisted view of fashion, and it excludes everyone except for a skinny, blonde, white girl. And unfortunate as it is to say, even those women are being abused by the fashion industry.

Everyone else is a joke and a mockery. When we see Asian women in fashion, their culture is disrespected. When we see Muslim women in fashion, their faith is taken as a joke. When we see Black women in fashion, their bodies and culture are fetishized.

It's almost as if the fashion industry is forcing what they want us to look like down our throats. They want to take away our individuality. It is painful to see that so many people who claim to be socially diverse fall into the trap of praising western fashion when over and over again, it has proven itself to be nothing but a sham. Often, smaller designers who are worth something are undermined, and their designs are stolen from these corporate fashion houses.

Yes, I have tremendous respect for the designers who came before me. These designers were innovative in their time—because they rejected mainstream ideas and what corporate fashion told them to like.

None of them looked at another designer and said, 'I like this. This is my aesthetic.' Instead, they challenged mainstream fashion with 'I don't like this. This is not my aesthetic'. That made them revolutionary. They didn't follow the norm; they rejected the trends and created what they wanted to wear.

However, these designers were only revolutionary in their time, and I'm not inspired by their European interpretation of African and Black culture. I respect that they designed from the heart and overcame the fashion industry's obstacles to create what they wanted. But I have to make my own path.

As a person born and raised in a culture often fetishized and abused by mainstream fashion, I've learned to appreciate the truth of my history. My designs are inspired by my own experiences, background, and the knowledge that I have as a Black woman.

I create clothing that relates to women like me. I create clothing that caters to the individual taste and perspective of the Black woman who often struggles to love herself and her culture.

A few years ago, I made a vow that I would not support luxury fashion, fast fashion, and 'branded' fashion because it robs from the true creatives who beg for support. Now, I support small businesses and up-and-coming designers like myself whenever I get the chance because I believe in their work. I believe in their aesthetic, and I believe in their philosophy.

During my time at FIT, I was able to see the creative process of many of my fellow peers, and I've come to learn that each of us has a unique voice.

My aesthetic will never be everyone's cup of tea, but I know many people who resonate with my designs. It took me some time to find my style, and truly, there were times when I doubted it because it didn't look like everyone else's.

You asked me what's my aesthetic. My aesthetic is staying true to myself, following my intuition, and never letting go of who I am.

I am a Black Woman, the Daughter of the Most-High. I am a chosen generation, a royal priesthood, a holy nation, God's own woman, who He has called out of darkness into His marvelous light.

I design to emancipate, enlighten, and empower.

Bread

Excerpt #2

Lucien circled me. He wasn't dressed for this world; his leather vest covered a loose-fitting cotton shirt, kept closed by a simple silver brooch with the City of Light's crest branded into the metal. He continued to circle me, his pointed ears flexing every now and again, as though he was listening. Listening through the wind for the embers scattered about.

He still looked the same after all these millennia with his golden-brown hair just a shade lighter than his complexion and pointed ears lined with silver and gold. Teeth as sharp as a viper's and skin as smooth as a copper coin—he did take pride in his appearance, just like the other demons.

If he wore the local clothes, he would look almost Egyptian—almost, because there was something about him that wasn't human—and people would know.

If Lucien had made his appearances to any of them, whether the Romans or the Egyptians, they would easily consider him a god, and I had no doubt that he already made himself one.

The ring on his finger, heavy and golden, already told me all I needed to know.

"I figured I would keep your company," Lucien said, then he flicked his tongue. A serpent was embroidered in the worn leather, green and yellow with bright red eyes. "I thought I would entertain you."

I didn't say anything. I wouldn't say anything because there was nothing to say.

The sky above was gray and the clouds hovered, gradually lowering itself until it was a thick fog that surrounded the both of us. I walked through the fog, trusting that my feet would take me where I wanted to go, but through the haze I saw a brook—clear water so smooth and rich I could see my own reflection.

Then, Lucien's shadowy figure appeared behind me when I stooped closer to see it—to run my fingers through it. Water splashed up on my feet, cooling my aching heels. Everything was heavy and unreal, but I'd gone so long without water that for a second, I almost didn't care. I still kept my fingers inside the cool water, contemplating whether I should drink—

"Well?" Lucien's voice hissed through the air.

I stood up, and slowly, the brook pulled away until the fog swallowed it up. "You're causing this," I said.

"You're hungry."

I turned to look the demon in his glittering eyes. He stooped to pick up a stone, red and dusty, then he handed it to me.

"If you are truly the son of God, turn this into bread."

My mouth was parched, but at the sight of the stone, it suddenly salivated—bread. I could … reach for it … and make myself something to eat….

"You are the son of God?" Lucien questioned, his eyebrow arching in anticipation of what I would do.

My fingers flexed at the stone he held—the stone that slowly morphed into something edible like what I would see in the market places that scattered the villages in the north. The stone—

"You do look worse than Yon," Lucien said. "He wandered around right here eating nothing but bugs." Lucien grinned. "But you—you are God. You are a part of the Divine Triune. You can do anything with the power you have."

The power I once had. The power I'd given up to come here. So, genuinely, I could do nothing. Nothing until I felt the prick of my fingers—embers coming back ever so lightly at the sight of a stone.

If I willed it just enough, just a little bit, I could try. It ran underneath my skin, not the explosion of pure energy that I was used to—red and brewing and burning—but it was there. The embers were there, and I wondered if Yah had somehow, between the time I'd been baptized and then come here to the desert, given it back to me.

My eyes flicked up to meet Lucien's and he smiled with his fangs still showing.

Years ago, I remembered what Simeon said. *'We don't need bread'*. We didn't. We'd spent the entire evening listening to the stories I'd told until our *Ima* had come home with something to eat.

Yah was greater than my *Ima*, than Simeon—than Lucien who stood in front of me as only he would. "Man cannot survive on bread alone," I said. And the stone rolled out his hand.

"What do you mean by that?" A snarl snapped in place on his face, almost feeling utterly defeated that he hadn't gotten me to turn his stone into bread.

That day, I'd told the younger siblings the story of the Hebrews, how they trekked through the wilderness hungry and starving, but Yah didn't leave them empty-stomached.

"Silly you. Quoting the scriptures."

Each day—each day I'd spend here for a year the Hebrews had spent living in the desert wandering around day and night. They didn't starve—when all they had was manna, they still pushed on. They ate, but they still complained. I would stay here to push through the blockades they couldn't push through—

Because if I was to be their Messiah—I had to prove it.

Reflect

As water reflects the face,
so does one's life reflects the heart.

Proverbs 27:19

The Letter

Dear Yeshua,

I have heard so much about You. You've done so many things for me and those around me that I couldn't help but notice. I must show my appreciation. I believe that You are my Savior. I recognize that You died for me. That was so brave of you to die for me.

It might have all been sad, but the good news is that You came back to life! I didn't know how else to thank You, so I wrote this letter instead.

Firstly, I must say that I have gotten so many things from You that I did not deserve, but it was so nice of You to give them to me anyway. I want to say thank You for all that. Secondly, You've answered my prayers. Sometimes, when I ask You for things, I feel silly because I always think of how I should pay You back, but then I remember that You had already paid for them on the cross, so I have to thank You for that too.

Lastly, You helped me out so much throughout life. You are really a blessing. If it weren't for You, I wouldn't be here today, so I thank You.

Now, I want to ask You: can You help me be more like You? You're the coolest person I've ever met: so smart, loving, and kind. I heard You came here already some two thousand years ago and so many people can't wait till You come back. So, I'm asking, can I be a bit more like You? Can You come live in me so that I can be a cool and fun person too?

If You do that for me, then that would be nice. And then I could be excited about Your coming too. It would be really nice to meet You in person.

Your biggest fan

P.S. When You come, can I get Your autograph? Oh wait, maybe You might give me something way better than that…

Nets

Excerpt #3

"If you wanted to incite a riot, you could," Andras teased as the crowds thinned out.

Most of the people had gone back to the market when the sun began to set, but I was too tired to notice the boats gradually drifting back to the shore.

Simon had already given up; he was slumped in the corner, his eyes red and strained from an entire day of disappointment. Ya'aqov, despite his slouched demeanor, was the happier one. He whistled a tune every now and again, reciting Psalms to himself—words he'd probably learned growing up, despite never reading a single thing in his life.

Only the five of us remained at the now-still lake. The boats gently rocked back and forth as the men pulled their nets up to the shore. "Still haven't caught anything?" I asked as I looked into the empty waters.

"Spent the whole night," Simon said as he strained to pull the nets further inland. "Still didn't catch anything."

I got up, drawing closer to the edge of the water. It was empty. The shallow edge of the lake proved to be useless, so I stepped back into the boat. A few tiny fish swam around and around, too small to ever get tangled in the nets. How lucky they were. "Have you tried going farther out?" I turned to look at Simon.

"We tried everything."

I grabbed one of the nets still sitting in the boat, handing it to him. "Take this."

He stared at me with questioning eyes, ready to laugh at my determination, but he took the net without saying anything. Simon stepped inside the boat, then turned to face me. "What are you planning to do?" The grit in his voice was jagged.

The sky was already darkening into hues of purple and reds. He didn't want to go back in the water, but I had a plan.

I scaled the entirety of the net until I found the other end, then I lowered myself into the water, swimming out to the other boat. When I slid out, Yochanan was already looking down into the water. He seemed more enthusiastic about going back—at least more than Simon.

I climbed into the boat, handing him the other end of the net.

"You know," he began, "I could've sailed closer to take it."

"I know." But somehow, the water felt comforting.

I stared into the water below. Still nothing. Not even a small wave formed or cracked up to the surface, and all those tiny fish I'd seen were long gone.

"Lower the nets," I called to Simon.

He furrowed his brows. "I told you we haven't caught a thing all day." He looked at the net in his hand. "Fine," he shouted back. "But only because it was you who asked."

He and Andras took their end of the nets and lowered it. Yochanan and Ya'aqov did the same. I stayed close to the edge of the boat, skimping my fingers across the water. But nothing. At the wedding, I'd felt just a tiny pinch of power snaking through my veins. Here, with my fingers dipped in the water, the spark returned a bit brighter, but not enough to attract any attention.

Soon, silver lights glowed from underneath the now-black lake. One entire day of empty nets meant I'd go an entire day without eating anything. Plus, if I wanted to convince these men to take the trip with me to Jerusalem, the least I could do was have food with me.

The fish they'd managed to catch was deplorable. It wasn't going to last even half a day, if so much.

"Lower," I said.

The men moved their boats further out into the lake, closing in on each other until a small pool formed between. Still nothing came up but the silver lights that flashed from my fingertips, swimming around in the water. Each minute that passed meant another minute of hunger, but I knew something was in the lake.

Whatever it was came closer and closer as the silver embers ignited under the night-filled water.

"How long is this going to take?" Simon whined as he tugged the nets.

"As long as it needs to take."

A whimper escaped his lips. "What do you need?" he asked. "You don't have to do all this; we can just go to the market and—"

"Hush." I thought I heard something. I let more than just the spark of energy escape from me—I flooded the entire lake with silver and gold lights. Just a bit more and then—

Fish.

The light glowed red in the darkness of the water below. No one else saw it. No one else saw the face that formed in the water. The face of a young boy who once stared at the water many eons ago before this universe was even made.

His eyes were bright and amber, his hair a reddish-brown that glowed underneath a sunlight that shadowed the heavens. He was all by himself on an island, his only friends being the birds and lizards who kept his company. Before he was given a Throne seated next to Yah, that boy was a lonely child wandering an island filled with only dreams.

Surrounded by sand and an ocean so blue, that boy had one little spark left underneath his nailbeds—a spark that would open up his world to a universe unexplored.

Every single animal on that island would come to him—because the spark he had gave them life. It was in his blood. They'd come to him with a song written in their hearts, only offering him the best of what they had. And when that young boy became a king, he never forgot those small, little creatures who found a home in his open arms.

I saw that boy staring at me. And soon, along with him, were several other fish coming until they gathered in schools so dense, the lake became a kaleidoscope of silvers, golds, turquoises, and blues.

That same boy had come to Earth to offer the humans the same hope and comfort he once offered to island-creatures. He no longer opened his arms to the animals who found solace in his embrace, but rather, he opened his arms to the people. He had something to give them. That something was in his blood—my blood could do that.

"Pull the nets up." I rested my arms of the edge of the boat, still staring at the many fish that flipped and fluttered around and around in the water.

As the men pulled the nets, the fish strained against the tired ropes. The nets cackled and creaked underneath all the fish that piled up on each other.

"Too much—" Yochanan strained the words. "Too much. Fish." His eyes squinted shut, but he kept one open just to see the fish leap into the boat, gleefully flopping about inside.

Ya'aqov was no better. He was already so strained, his skin turned red as sweat bubbled on his skin. "Why. So. Much?" The thrill in his voice—either for the fish or for me—echoed into the night sky.

When the nets finally gave out and snapped, all the fish flopped into Yochanan's boat. Simon and Andras steered their boat closer, pulling more fish into theirs. Simon stared at me. He had no words.

"The boat is sinking," Andras said. "Pull into shore."

"We can't. We're too deep—" Ya'aqov dropped his words, staring around him in awe. "We're in the shallow." He stepped out of the boat and gave a small leap. "We're in the shallow!" His small chuckle pealed into laughter.

Yochanan steered the boat closer to the shore, and I hopped out, taking as much fish with me as possible.

"My lord." Simon dropped to his knees. I was tempted to crouch with him, to pull him back on his feet, but then he began, "I'm too sinful a man for you to be around."

I was alarmed—not confused—but alarmed.

His brother had done the same, until one by one, all four men were on their knees semi-circling me. I wanted to think it was a joke—they were known for the games they pulled on each other, but when I saw Ya'aqov's tear-stained face, I realized they were genuine.

"You are the one Yon spoke of," Simon said. "How is it that you still stay with us?"

"Simon." I grabbed his arm, pulling him to his feet. "Follow me."

The other three stood up as well, grabbing their tunics that laid mindlessly in the sand. "Where?" Andras asked.

"Come with me, and I will make you fishers of men."

The four of them stared on, speechless.

Yochanan pulled his tunic on, raking the fish into one of the buckets he had. "Wherever you go, we will go as well."

White Light Zenith

When you become short-tempered;
Suppress it with long-suffering
When you become full of hatred;
Still be gentle
When you become frustrated;
Have patience
When you become heartless;
Remember to have compassion
Do not let the red anger overpower you
For the gift of God is full of power and abides in you

When you become envious;
Be content
When you become deceitful;
Remember the truth
When you become a liar;

Always be honest
When you become insincere;
Remain trustworthy
Do not let the orange greed overpower you
For the gift of God is filling and abides in you

When you become depressed;
Still sing with joy
When you become hopeless;
Still have hope
When you are feeling pain;
Maintain your health
When you go through suffering;
Still endure
Do not let the yellow sadness overpower you
For the gift of God is joy and the joy of the Lord is
your strength

When you become anxious;
Have a sound mind
When you become hysterical;
Remain loving
When you become emotionless;
Remain affectionate
When you become cold-hearted;
Be temperate
Do not let the green fear overpower you
For the gift of God is love, abide in love and nothing
shall harm you

When you become desperate;

Remain at peace
When you become detached;
Walk in unity
When you are friendless;
Still be friendly
When you feel lifeless;
Keep your spirit lively
Do not let the blue loneliness overpower you
For the gift of God is the Comforter and he shall
comfort you

When you become arrogant;
Be humble
When you become stubborn;
Keep an open mind
When you become selfish;
Remain selfless
When you become haughty;
Still submit
Do not let the purple pride overpower you
For the gift of God is humility. Be humble, and he will
lift you up

When you become obsessive;
Exercise self-control
When you become perverted;
Remain pure
When you become lewd;
Remain intimate with God
When you become unfaithful;
Walk by faith, not by sight

Do not let the pink lust overpower you
For the gift of God is pure; have faith in God

59

Do not let the pink lust overpower you
For the gift of God is pure; have faith in God

River Woman

No one knew who she was, except they only saw her at the Rosa River at noon. She wasn't special or anything. She looked like the typical woman in the villages: straight, long, shiny black hair, skin the color of caramel sweets, and body as tall as a plush European model, around five feet ten.

They just found it strange that she'd always sit under orchids and towering cherry trees that blossomed so many pink flowers that you'd think the trees were pink. She would place her feet inside the icy-cold streams that reflected the cherry trees' vibrant pink color.

She was always at Rosa River.

No one knew who she was, except they all thought she was strange.

But not Eleanor.

Eleanor thought the woman was a mermaid. Eleanor was only five years old, so they couldn't blame her for her bright imagination. Still, they all had their suspicions and their fanciful superstitions. It was just that Eleanor was the only one who dared say it out loud.

The woman had the slender legs of a human, but no one was ever sure. No one was ever sure about the woman by the river.

Today, however, Eleanor had slipped out of her mother's house to go to Rosa River. She wanted to see the woman. Even though the river was stunning, it was dangerous. Its rushing streams had a tendency to climb the banks, threatening to flood the nearby village. It never did.

Today, when Eleanor slipped out, her mother knew she'd gone by the river. She pushed her things to the side, rushing to find her daughter, but when she got to the river, no one was there. Desperate, she pleaded for help. The neighbors heard her calls and set out searching the banks.

But Eleanor was there.

They simply couldn't see her searching for the woman. She tried to keep near the river without slipping on the moss-covered boulders, but Eleanor's tiny feet held no grip, and no matter how much she tried, she still slipped. Her reflexes were sharp, even for her age, and she managed to clutch onto a nearby branch. She swung herself on land, falling on the dewy grass, then she slipped through the cherry trees as fast as her tender legs could carry her. All she wanted to do was ask the woman for her name, but the excitement had taken over, leaving Eleanor trembling like a lone leaf in the storm.

She grabbed one of the tree trunks, but it was too wide for her, and the moss was too slippery for her fingers. Again, she fell into the river.

She desperately tried to keep her head above the icy rapid, but she couldn't. The river was strong—the river was determined to keep her under. Then, through her weak eyes, she saw a figure approaching her, tall and slender, with hair that cascaded from behind her.

"Ma!" she cried, but the figure didn't respond. Closer and closer, the silhouette came until Eleanor could see who it was—the river woman! Her weakened eyes began to close on her, but with the last light that peered through, she smiled at the sight of the woman coming closer. The woman grabbed her wrist, pulling her out of the river.

Her eyes opened, then she met the face of the sunbaked woman. How it glistened under the sun. Her eyes were dark and lovely, and something silver glistened underneath the richness of their color. Eleanor finally closed her eyes, taking in the scent of salt and sea breeze, her last thought carefully knitting itself around her.

The woman by the river.

Opinion

A fool takes no pleasure in understanding,
But only expressing his opinion.

Proverbs 18:2

Finding Black

When something is 'black', oftentimes it is associated with 'bad' or 'evil'.

No one wants to have a 'black' personality and many find it weird that someone's favorite color may be black. However, these days black seems to take on a more positive attribute. Black means power or authority. Hidden or concealed. Mystery. Those in the highest positions are given a 'black' card.

Black absorbs all things; all colors.

Some say that black is the absence of color or the absence of light. What they really mean to say is that black does not reflect color but rather absorbs it.

It means that black is all colors. So why is black evil?

Because we perceive darkness to be black. But this far from the truth.

Darkness is actually the absence of light. But darkness is not black. Darkness is not a color. Darkness is bad.

However, black is a different thing entirely. It absorbs light. It is the result of all colors mixed together, creating something powerful, something unique. Something black.

Brace Yourself

Not everyone finds candies sweet
Not everyone finds lemons sour
But everyone knows that love is strong
And it is in love, you have invincible power

Favor by another isn't always right
And despise isn't always wrong
But standing up for yourself in times of trouble
Proves to others that you are strong

In cases where the fire is burning hot
And the ice is freezing cold
Then it is a risk you have to take
And it you come out well, you come out bold

Always be courageous, never fear

Be bold, stand tall, don't let words bring you down
Sticks and stones may break your bones
But words will always stick around

Brace yourself for the upcoming battle
Brace yourself for the fight
For if you win, you'll have victory that says:
"Darkness was overcome by light."

Not everyone finds the royal in purple
Not everyone finds the calm in blue
But people cherish the most perfect moments
When they find love in you

Love the Color

It is probably hard to explain where I draw the line between my love for pink and my love for black.

Let's get it clear: I do love pink—specifically neon pink. I find it to be a uniquely weird color that is hard to find in things that I use daily. Or at least, it adds a bit of color to my complex life.

But that is exactly where I draw the line: pink items. No, I don't want to live in a pink house or drive a pink car or paint my room pink. All of that looks hideous to me. I would prefer to drink from a pink glass maybe, or collect oddly satisfying pink stationery like staplers, hole punchers, notebooks and whatever else.

I am a person who likes pattern, especially the more 'alternative' ones, and anything that doesn't necessarily confirm to a particular color scheme.

With that being said, I hate when people get the idea that my entire world will be pink. Oddly enough, however, I love black even more than I love pink. It is the black that gets to me.

I love black clothing, black cars, black décor, and anything black to me seems like the most beautiful and exotic thing ever.

There is something powerful about black. Something commanding and unique. Black to me is more than just a 'color'. It is a representation of the inner self. The mystery, the depth—the soul.

Black has become one of the most 'rejected' yet 'respected' colors in society. It's reserved for only the best. Many would wonder 'why black?' but I will tell you why.

It is only in the Western world we are taught that black is bad. We go to funerals in black but we wear white at weddings. The misconception is that we think that is how it always was. But it's not. Someone changed it.

Black was actually a popular wedding color before Queen Victoria decided to change the trend and wear a white wedding dress. In other cultures, reds, golds, and blues were the staple wedding colors. White in eastern cultures is actually reserved for funerals.

I draw the line to how black is represented in our culture.

As a matter of fact, I believe the association of 'black being bad' has stemmed from slavery. That's not to say that things can't get better, but why should black be bad? Why should only wealthy people enjoy what black gives to them, while everyone else lives under the false assumption that anything black is evil?

I say embrace the black.

Black is everything. It represents beauty, diversity, strength, and power.

Black is the absorption of all the colors we know. So, if you love black just like me, then you'd appreciate the color in everything. It is what black is. And once you go black, you can never go back.

I Still Have You

In any case, lost or found
I still have you
And maybe with our friendship gone
I still have you
Out of love, I found the perfect one
I still have you
Till beauty dies and ugly comes
I still have you
Swinging on the porch swing, singing songs
I still have you
And if I run away, I'll run in your arms
I still have you
While it makes me cry when I see broken hearts
I know your love is true
Till death we part, but that's so wrong

'cause I still have you
Sit by your grave and smile because
I still have you...

Alabaster

EXCERPT #4

The aroma of rain penetrated the walls, soaking the room in something sweet and comforting. There was a hint of something metallic—almost like copper, but not quite as cold and overbearing as I knew it should've been.

At the other end of the table, the men chatted away, thick in laughter and conversation, but outside, the rain poured down in great heaps—whatever had angered the sky above didn't seem to bother the men.

But it bothered me.

A light fragrance dressed the air, blending into the rain's own distinct odor: dirt and something strong; I couldn't quite identify it.

Dining with a Pharisee was rare, but Nathaniel and Phillip had insisted that we stay over by a friend of theirs. Though the discomfort poked at me, it was better than clutching together under a narrow canopy, hiding from the downpour of rain.

The laughter now ceased, the door creaking open, echoing the sound of cracking bones. Simon, the host Pharisee, turned his head toward the door, and I traced his line of sight.

"What is she doing here?" he snarled.

Mariah slipped inside, closing the door behind her. She didn't address Simon or even look in his direction. She simply pulled the shawl that covered her hair off and threw it on the ground. Her arms were lined with gold and silver bracelets, and on two of her fingers were simple rings. On her fifteenth birthday, Laz had given her those rings, and she wore them ever since.

The men grumbled among themselves, with Cephas poking me in the side to do something about Mariah. She'd been missing for the week and it bothered me that I couldn't find her, but the men were relieved that she wasn't trailing them, and for that, I didn't bring it up.

Maybe I should have.

She didn't seem too enthralled to be left out of such a splendid occasion, but the bruises that her bracelets hid told me a different story.

My stomach dropped.

Her eyes met with mine, and when I traced the line of her fingers, I saw that she clutched a jar—of perfume. It wasn't the one she said Elisheva had given to her.

It was different. It was larger, more expensive. Its fragrance had elevated the room, but staining it was blood. I could see it from where I sat—the red plastered all around the neck of the jar, on her fingers.

Mariah took each step with caution. Her tear-stained face was light and puffy, but it somehow radiated hope. The men were probably more than upset that she stalked us here, but I welcomed her presence. I promised her I would keep her safe.

It was a promise I wasn't going to turn my back on.

Mariah looked at the men seated around the table, then she turned toward me. Her feet were bare, her clothing tattered, her hands stained with henna and blood. The blood was caked into her skin, down to her toes. The cracks and scars she endured were her battle wounds that she'd worn proudly.

But today, something dreadful draped over her.

Closer she came until she stood right in front of me. The silence in the room drooped down like heavy storm clouds, yet, I felt every whisper that bounced off the walls. Each step Mariah took was more painful than the last—I felt it. When she was close enough, she only stared.

Her eyes were flooded with tears and all the things I didn't want to imagine. Then...

She broke the jar.

Shards of alabaster littered the floor, the perfume escaping from its prison as it danced freely in the rain-touched air. Drips of oil ran down my face into my beard—onto my lips.

The aroma was sweeter than the rain, than the roses that grew all around the small house I'd grown up in. It masked the blood, the pain, the anger that swelled inside her. It ran like tiny streams making its way down and down, burning everything in its path like a refiner's fire, polishing silver till it gleamed with the perfect reflection of the woman who stood in front of me.

It tasted of fire. It tasted of the purest olive oil that could be pressed and sold to the wealthiest man who lived in Judea.

It cascaded down into pools on the floor underneath my feet. Golden like honey, and somehow capturing the little hope that dwindled in Mariah's eyes as she tried to choke back the tears.

It relieved the tension that tugged on my heart, and eased the sore shoulders that carried the weight of the world. And when the last drop fell, it wiped away the tear that stained her face.

She wasn't finished.

The silence drew in like dark draperies across an open archway, but the muttering grew louder. And more poisonous.

Mariah's brown eyes were fixed on me, then she slipped to her knees, her sobbing drowning the silence that clung to the air.

I could—I could fix a broken heart. I could restore an untethered soul.

It was what I came here to do.

But something bitter climbed up my throat, leaving my mouth dry. What could I say? She was kneeling before me with tears drowning her face, her skin red and clammy to the touch, her eyes wet—her heart bleeding.

What could I do?

When all she had left was broken, she came to me with the pieces, hoping that I'd put them together like the puzzle of alabaster shards that lay at my feet. And when the unspoken questions flooded the room, my heart caved. Who else could heal the broken heart that bled on my feet, each drop of blood burning like the perfume that washed my skin?

And when no one else answered, I found that it was me.

Her breath danced in the air; her tears could fill the ocean of glass Yah had shown me years before I began this journey. I wanted to wipe those tears away. Those tears had a rune written inside them—one that only I understood. Those tears were written in a language only I could speak, and to leave her here, relentless and crying—it would be cruel.

All I could do was lift her chin up so that her eyes met mine. I saw into the deep brown pool of pain. "Mariah," I said, letting each word coat her like a silken chiffon scarf, bright red and comforting like the satin she wore and twirled around in the first day I'd met her.

This time it finally broke her.

In her eyes, I saw what she'd given up for this bottle of perfume—who she gave it to.

She shook violently in my grasp, but she held onto me as though I was the only branch left for her to catch before falling to an imminent death.

"Does he know what sort of woman she is? What sort of woman he has touching her?" Simon whispered to the other guests in the house.

Yes, I did.

Mariah had sauntered into his house, uninvited. She plodded through the rain, her skin caked in blood and dirt. Mariah watched him and said nothing. She knew what he'd done to her—what she'd given up simply because her brother was in pain. Nothing but hatred was written on his face. He'd kept his sins buried so deep in his heart, the mass that sat right above it was black and hardened and as cold as a miller's stone.

His bitter gaze slid over Mariah—a gaze that was once filled with lust was now repulsed by the sight of her. His eyes dared her to say something, but her tears had already told me. Her guilt stained her fingers, but she did whatever she could to wash it all away.

His guilt stained his heart—and he did whatever he could to bury it.

I let Mariah go as she curled up at the foot of the chair. "Simon," I said, turning my attention to him. "I have something I want to tell you."

The pharisee straightened himself, giving me his full attention. "Tell me."

"Suppose two men owed money to a moneylender. One owed five hundred denarii, and the other owed only fifty, but neither had the money to pay him back. So, the moneylender decided to forgive both debts. Who do you think would love the moneylender more?"

Simon scoffed at the question. "The one who owed the most."

"You are right." I brought Mariah to her feet, then let her sit next to me as the men watched pitifully.

Her gaze softened into something lighter, the burdens of her tears now gone.

"This woman," I said to him, "Did more for me in these few minutes, than you have done since I came here. She wet my feet with her tears and wiped them with her hair, but you didn't even offer to wash my feet as the custom.

"She broke perfume over me, but you have yet to put oil on my head. And as I sat here, she has not stopped kissing me, but you haven't greeted me since. Her many sins, which you accuse her of, have been forgiven, and for that, she showed me great love. But whoever has been forgiven little, loves very little."

Simon returned his gaze to her, the hatred swelling in his eyes even more. The last tear loosened from her eye.

I turned to Mariah, taking her in my embrace. "Your sins are forgiven."

"Who are you to forgive sins," Simon snapped. The other men held their tongue, but in their hearts, I knew they'd taken his side.

But … if he only knew….

I Am The Black Woman

I was captured from my home

Brought to a land unknown

Stripped of my power and robbed of my wealth

Captured in chains, drained of my health

Given over to heathens who lied to my face

Who took my innocence and called me 'disgrace'

Left with no identity, I searched for a name

Only to find a life riddled with pain

Left with no path, I carved my own way

Left with no option, I struggled each day

I was left unappreciated, desolated for my skin

A skin too black to ever fit in

Against all odds, I rose above the sea

Swam against the tides, just to set me free

On either side of the shore, I was met with only hate

But I never let the waters drown my faith

I kept paddling till I saw a land of gold

I rowed against the currents to see the truth unfold

When life let me down, I held my head up high

Because my crown will only stay on if I looked to the sky

I saw in heaven the many faces that died to see me live

I saw in heaven the Creator and the promises He fulfilled

In this skin as black as night, I saw promises of hope

I saw promises of love, forgiveness, and growth

I saw the truth and my identity written in my skin

I saw the story of who I was written in melanin

My eyes were opened and I saw my history

I saw who I am now, and who I'm meant to be

From my womb I birthed the human race

From my DNA, all people came to shape

I am created to only elevate

I am created to become great

I am who I am in Yah: God with all power

I am the Black Woman who will never cower

I am who I am in the God of all creations

I am the Black Woman who brought forth the nations

ACKNOWLEDGMENTS

I began working on my thesis collection, I AM THE BLACK WOMAN, in the last semester of college. It was a culmination of everything I'd done in college so far. It was supposed to be the highlight of all my work, a tribute to myself for a job well-done.

Instead, it became a story I told through prose and poetry. From words lifted off the pages of my heart, I finally gathered them together and placed them here, in a book.

I dedicate this book to every woman who feels as though she lost her identity. To every woman who feels let down, rejected, oppressed, objectified, used, abused, hurt, ignored—this is for you.

Remember, you are God's creation. You are fearfully and wonderfully made.

Get More!

Check out the latest in the *Kingdoms of Yah* series on Amazon.

- The Bloodlust Power
- The Ruby Insignia

Coming Soon:

- The Illaryian Vow
- Kingdoms of Yah Book Four**

**Look out for the title by signing up to my mailing list

Check out all my books by visiting **thepinkravyn.com** or scanning the QR Code below.

Don't miss out on the latest releases such as:

- The Aroma of Rain (preorder in 2023)
- The Elēda Series

Sign up to my mailing list by scanning the QR code below: